The
Journey
Before
Success

Transparent Lessons Of A Saved Woman

Jeanna Adowa Brodie-Mends

Published by

Peaches

Publications

Published in London by Peaches Publications, 2022.

www.peachespublications.co.uk

Images courtesy of Pixabay.

British Library Cataloguing in Publication Data: A catalogue record for this book is available from the British Library.

ISBN: 9798838824677.

Book cover design: Peaches Publications LTD.

Typesetter: Winsome Duncan.

Editor: Mary Cindell.

Proofreader: Virginia Rounding.

Table of Contents

Disclaimer

This is a recollection based on my memories and experience. Some real names have been changed to respect the identity of those concerned.

Dedication

*This book is dedicated to the woman who loved me
without condition – my nanny,
Carlotta Oneata Moore
(19.3.1943 –19.4.2019).*

*I am so pleased that I got to honour her with our Women of
Excellence 'Rainbow in the Cloud' award in March 2019.*

*Unfortunately, she transitioned the following month,
on 19th April 2019.*

The Journey Before Success

Acknowledgements

I want to give thanks to the Almighty Creator, my ancestors (family members who have passed on before us) and Spirit for guiding me and protecting me on my Journey Before Success.

I want to thank me! – Jeanna Adowa Brodie-Mends, for never giving up on yourself, for showing yourself unconditional love, for being your own best friend, for the willingness to feel the fear and do it anyway. For your continuous ability to remain grounded and demonstrate strength through the many adversities you have faced. For being willing to break any archetype of glass ceiling or box, for operating in your true power and doing the work on and within yourself to know who you are. I salute you, as you are a true Woman of Excellence who continues to show up as her authentic self, No Matter What! and for always remembering that without the Almighty Creator nothing is possible.

I want to acknowledge my nanny; although we weren't blood-related, she was the best nanny I could ask for. One person in the world who loved me unconditionally while giving me direction and support. We spent so much time together; we would drink, watch old western films, listen to music, go out to random places on our drives and shopping.

The Journey Before Success

We had a really beautiful relationship and would talk at least three times a day.

We travelled around the world together, visiting Canada, Barbados and St Lucia in 2018. St Lucia was my nan's last trip, and it was a surprise. I just booked the ticket and then asked her to read the message. She was shocked, but you could see the joy on her face.

We shared so many cherished moments together; even in my nan's passing, she was still thinking about me. I will never forget sharing her cheese sandwich and cup of tea that night in the hospital. A love lost.

To the three Black Kings in my life, the awesome Andwele, Emmanuel and Lutumba. Your continued encouragement, love and support towards me on my journey have been truly invaluable, and I thank you all for being so imperfectly perfect. While writing this I realised that you are all younger than me, lol. Very wise men indeed.

I would like to acknowledge my mum, Marina Julien, the matriarch of our family. You provided my first blueprint on what it means to be a businesswoman, to be an entrepreneur. Through your work in your factory, I learned how to identify and create wealth by looking at the material pieces around the factory and the cabs we would take and

The Journey Before Success

seeing that the cab drivers could benefit from having a small string bag to put their loose change in instead of the ashtray. That was my first product created and successfully sold.

Today I am using some of those same skills in my business and supporting others to realise their dreams and goals.

To my dad, Daniel Amissa Brodie-Mends, a typical African father always going on about education from a very young age. You always said education is the key! You said no matter what anyone takes from me, they cannot take what is in my mind. I thank you for giving me the information, determination and focus to continue studying and always wanting to grow and learn more.

I would like to acknowledge Mr DOK, who is the man I was married to. Whilst we had our ups and downs, he was one of my best friends right till the end. He was a man of many words; anyone who knew him knew that he was very poetic. He was loving, very caring and a good listener. Mr DOK had a passion to light the candle of potential in the minds of young people which he did very well: Mr DOK, a true Descendant Of Kings.

To my beautiful daughter-in-love, Kairi Weekes-Sanderson, also known as Melody. That is what I call her because she has a beautiful voice, and basically creates music and brings peace and love wherever she goes. Kairi is a ray of sunshine. Our relationship has always been very transparent and has grown from strength to strength. We create so many beautiful memories through our joint passion for travelling. We have visited Portugal, Barbados and Cuba together. I'm so proud of the woman that you are and the woman that you are going to become, and the many people's lives you will impact. I love you, Kai Kai xx.

My beautiful niece, La Braya, thank you for giving me the motivation and the vision to create a better world for those who follow in our footsteps. You're such a beautiful soul, you're beautiful on the outside, but definitely, you're beautiful, even more so on the inside. Your compassionate love for other people inspires me to do the work that I do. You are so precious to my journey. Thank you so much for smiling through the hard times, always encouraging and being the example of true love in action, my precious Bray Bray and uncle DOK's crazy frog.

Thank you to all my sisters and brother for your support and encouragement over the years. We were brought up to know that our siblings are our first friends. We share so many beautiful memories – of stealing meat from the pot, flying up the stairs when one of us switched off all the lights, to getting licks for our wrongdoings.

The Journey Before Success

I have to give a special acknowledgement to my sister Joyclen for being my shield and protection from when I was born, and you still try to protect me now. Not that I listen all the time, but I do appreciate and love you.

To all my nieces, nephews and godchildren, you are all a driving force for me to complete my journey the best I possibly can, and when I transition, I will leave empty, as I will have ensured I've poured all that I had into the lives that need it.

And to my friends who are my family, I truly appreciate and love you all. For being my support even when I didn't recognise I needed the support. For not telling me what you thought I wanted to hear but what I needed to hear. For giving me the space to live my life without judgement and with unconditional love.

My beautiful Peace … thank you for being my cheerleader and a visual reminder of why I do what I do. I'm so proud of your willingness to continue to show up for yourself. You hold up a mirror that reminds me of who I am. Love you, girl xx.

Thank you to Mr Dawkins, otherwise known as Fisher, for being one of my first mentors. We would go on drives and the talks that we had really made an impact in my life. You showed me how to look to the future, to look at the direction I want to go, how to stay focused to think outside of the box and you showed me that there are always options.

Thank you to the women and men who have supported me on my Journey Before Success. Those who have helped to keep me on my toes. Those who have encouraged me when I felt I could not keep on going on and those who were honest. Those who didn't just tell me what they thought I wanted to hear, but were really honest.

I have to say a HUGE thank you to those of you who left me out at sea in the most turbulent years of my life! – to navigate the storms of life to find my own way back to shore!!! That has been the BIGGEST LESSON of my life to date.

'When people show you who they are, believe them the first time.' – Maya Angelou

Introduction

'Babu moments' is what I call my
ah-ha moments.

Moments when you get a mindset shift that you didn't see coming. A thought that creates a spark in you, getting you energised, focused, determined and ready to take decisive action with precision. No area is left uncovered. For me, Babu came as a result of me having my own ah-ha moment during a conversation with a friend and instead of saying 'ok babes I hear you', predicted text typed 'Babu'. We both laughed and from that point on I have used Babu to identify my own ah-ha moments.

Your Babu moment is your connection to a thing, person(s) or place that makes you say, 'Yes! This makes so much sense.'

Throughout this book, there are numerous calls to action, encouraging you to take action – take the step, no matter how small: just do it!

The Journey Before Success

Actually, let's see how many Babu moments you can identify on YOUR Journey Before Success.

Let's start now...

List at least seven Babu moments you have experienced during your last year. Feel free to post them on your social media and tag me in *@annaej_coaching*.

Within this book, we're going to get very clear on your truth. If there is nothing else that you do in your life, you should always be honest, at least with yourself.

We will look to identify your vision as we answer: How do you know what your vision is? How do you know what your purpose is? Too often, I ask people the question, 'Do you know your purpose? What do you want to achieve in the world?' Typically, their answer is: 'I do not know, Jeanna.'

This book will give you some key steps on how to actually materialise and start to see that vision for yourself because, once we have seen it, our imagination and our brain are so powerful. Once we have seen the vision, we know that we can manifest it into reality. I know that word 'manifest' is thrown around a lot – manifesting this, manifesting that – but it is true: if you have seen it, it can happen.

We're going to look at forgiveness. How are we showing up for ourselves in the world? Are we carrying around the weight of other people? Are we creating hurdles and stumbling blocks on our Journey Before Success?

To attain clarity in my life, I focused on three things I value most – my Choices, Freedom and Lifestyle. As we review your Journey Before Success, we'll definitely be looking at ways that you can make those choices for your own clarity, knowing who you are, your truth, and then living it out.

Once you decide you're going to make that decision to love yourself, you'll be able to say how you're going to live freely and live the lifestyle of your choosing. It may be that you want to create all these amazing memories and experiences so that when you're older, you can look back on them with a smile. Or decide that you do not want to get to the end of your life with regrets and saying: 'Why didn't I do this?'

I remember one time going to The Gambia, and I received donations from a church that I was attending at the time, and a few of the people who donated said, 'You know what, Jeanna, I'm actually envious of you, because I wish I had done this when I was younger.' And it just made me look at them and think, 'I do not want to be at a point in my life where I'm living with regret.'

This book is to encourage you to go for it. Just go! – just do it. Do not waste time. Do not procrastinate. Do not think, oh, maybe later, or when this happens, then you're going to do it. Just do it now! If it is something that you want to do, it will always work out as it should.

'Nothing that is for you will ever pass you.'
– Andwele

The Journey Before Success

We're going to look at how you can identify and set macro goals that you want to achieve in your life, then break them down into smaller micro bite-sized steps.

'Every journey begins with your first step.'
– Jeanna

I encourage you to use this toolkit, learn from it, take what is for you, digest it, and put the toolkit down. You do not have to read it in any particular order. Pick the lessons that are relevant to you, then apply it. Put it down, come back, pick it up again, and see where you can make improvements, because the reality is that this toolkit is about transformation, and there should always be continued growth throughout your life.

You should aim to always see change as you continue to apply the steps, principles and Babu moments that you are going to identify while using this toolkit throughout your journey – whether it is the first time you go through the toolkit, the second time or third.

The Journey Before Success

Be open to the process. Do not shut yourself off and think that is not possible. There is nothing impossible. Anything is possible.

If you are someone of faith, use your go-to scriptures that underpin your faith. For me, it is Jeremiah 29:11 – "For I know the plans I have for you," declares the Lord.' With this, no matter what I see before me, I know that if it is not what I had visioned, it will pass. 'This too shall pass.' It is not going to remain here. And that gives me the encouragement to get over or find a way through.

If you are not of faith, you may choose to use positive affirmations and stand on the power of your words. Affirmations of 'I am powerful. I am strong. I am unique. I have a purpose.' Do not shut off with negative self-talk.

Remember, many people have different journeys, and everyone's journey is suitable for them. There is no one-size-fits-all. Be open to newness because when we are closed off, that means we are creating limitations for ourselves. There is NO glass ceiling; we have smashed everything on the ceiling. We are not within a box as the box does NOT even exist!

As you begin this toolkit, think of yourself as walking into this journey with a blank canvas. I'll even encourage you to get a sheet of paper or your journal – whatever it is that you're going to use to write down and take notes as you start your Journey Before Success.

When people begin their Journey Before Success, the first question I always ask them or what I ask them to think about is: 'Who am I?' So let me just tell you who I am.

As I started to write this book, my name was Jeanna Brodie-Mends Sanderson, and I am a woman of African and Caribbean descent. My father is from West Africa. His dad was from Ghana, his mum was from Sierra Leone, and he was born in Nigeria.

The Journey Before Success

My mum is from Dominica in the Caribbean, and I was born in East London. I have a mix of many different cultures. Being brought up in the East End, which is considered a deprived area of London, there was a lot of stigma. I remember times when people would say not to put your postcode on your CV because people looked at you differently.

I was brought up Christian, although we had our African traditions. I realised from the age of 7 that I was not like anybody else and did not have to be limited in how I express or show up in the world. Knowing this gave me the freedom to know that I could be an individual when other people said I had to be the same. It made me identify and recognise blessings, even when things looked broken or times when we weren't necessarily the most well-off family.

I remember times when my mum would purchase a packet of biscuits we called the broken biscuits. The packet had different biscuits, and I would take out maybe a handful and put aside the ones that looked a bit more perfect. And then I'd taste them, wondering where they came from. This experience as a child inspired my desire to travel, meet new people, have new experiences and create beautiful memories. As a child I was able to envision it; as an adult it has become my reality.

I share this with you to show you that, no matter your circumstances, you do not have to conform and live up to the stigma or the stereotype others may choose to label you with. If you have a vision that is greater than your environment, do that. You go for it. And I just hope that, by utilising this toolkit, you will be inspired to take those action steps in every area of your life. You can have a dream, but if you do not take action, that is all it is. You can have beautiful ideas, but if you do not take action, they are just ideas. You need to take action for it to become your life experience. And I promise that you will enjoy it.

For myself, I'm living life on my terms. I make no excuses for the way that I live or the choices I make. I know what my vision and goals are and what my purpose is. I walk with my head held high; yes, there will be ups and downs, but that is inevitable in life. This is inevitable on your Journey Before Success. So do not be discouraged. I would encourage and implore you to continue taking the necessary action steps required to be the best version of yourself. Take the action required to show up for those that you want to leave your legacy for. We can walk around aimlessly in life, but by now, I know this isn't you. This cannot be you as you are a go-getter; you are reading this toolkit, getting prepared for dynamic transformation.

By the time you get to the end of this toolkit, there is no way you should still be walking around unaware of your purpose or how to show up for yourself. I encourage you to show up for yourself. Set intentional time aside and continue on your Journey Before Success, NO MATTER WHAT!!!

The Journey Before Success

I look forward to seeing the many, many things that you achieve and accomplish throughout your life. And I look forward to connecting with you.

The Journey Before Success

Sesa Wo Suban

Life Transformation, Growth and Renewal

This symbol combines two separate adinkra symbols. The 'Morning Star' placed inside the wheel identifies a new start to the day, while the wheel represents rotation or independent movement.

The Journey Before Success

The Journey Before Success

Lesson 1:
The Rabbit Hole

In 2016, I evicted myself from the rabbit hole. I say rabbit hole in the sense that I was in a very dark and low place. Similar to Alice in Wonderland when she went down the rabbit hole when she was falling and falling and falling. I was travelling around the world and continuing to support people in communities in the UK, the Caribbean and Africa.

From the outside, looking in, I was excelling in every area. I was married, in what appeared to be a very good marriage. I was in three different ministries within the church and had fantastic relationships with family members. Yet, I was in a very dark place and I was very comfortable in the rabbit hole. As I like cocktails, I always describe my experience in the rabbit hole as me sitting there on a deck chair, very comfortable, my Mojito cocktail in hand and spotlights all around me. I was very comfortable in that dark place. At times I even felt like I was having so much fun.

It took me to sit still one day to realise that this isn't where I'm supposed to be. I had a Babu moment.

'Jeanna, you're not actually living out your purpose. Where have you gone?' The question 'Who am I?' would always come up. At that moment, I could not answer truthfully that I am Jeanna, which made me stop to think. Where has Jeanna gone?

When I was about 15 years old, my mum was on benefits. In the UK, you get social security and child benefit for each child in the household. Every Monday, I remember queuing up to get that payment for my mum. I remember looking through the book and seeing my name in the book and thinking, 'Well, this is mine, as my name is here in the book, but I do not get it as spending money.' I said to my mum, 'It says Jeanna here – shouldn't I receive it?' That didn't necessarily go down too well with my mum, but nonetheless she said, 'Okay, you can have it in your own name.' We made an agreement and I put it into my name and could receive it directly.

However, when I went to queue up to cash the same benefits cheque, I was uncomfortable, even though for many years I had been collecting the money for the family. I didn't feel comfortable receiving it for myself, and that is when I realised this isn't where my life is going to be.

During my rabbit hole experience, I reminded myself of 15-year-old Jeanna, who made a choice to live a particular way. The three strands I stand on are Choice, Freedom and Lifestyle, and I found that when people were in receipt of benefits, I felt they were limited and dictated to on how they could spend the money, and this determined the type of lifestyle they could have.

In 2016 aged 37, I finally decided that enough was enough, and I was ready to evict myself from this rabbit hole. I chose to use my voice and feet to show up for myself and I walked out of that space with my head held high and my shoulders back. I got on a flight to Dubai to celebrate my friend's birthday as this was the outlet I needed. It was fantastic out there. When I was there, I remember saying, 'Oh, this is how the other half lives', and something caught me again – I would often say it is my spirit. It made me realise, 'Well, actually, Jeanna, you keep saying this.' At that moment, I realised maybe I'm actually the other half, because I always seem to be in an environment where I say the other half lives.

That trip spoke to me, telling me: 'Jeanna, this is where you're supposed to be. These are the things that you're supposed to be doing, do not ever forget that.' Dubai helped me revise my life and gave me the driving force to continue pushing forward.

The Journey Before Success

The realisation

I often say to people walking in their truth, what is your truth? Where are you now? Do not be concerned with how it sounds or appears to anyone else; what is your truth?

When we get clarity on what needs to be done and a person accepts their truth, I say to them, 'Now, the next step is that you need to forgive yourself, because the reality is you chose to be in that space.'

Everyone has a choice, no matter how hard it is. Ultimately, people choose to remain in spaces, both good and bad, for many complex reasons. I do not say it lightly, that it is easy or that people can just walk away from situations. For example, I stayed in that dark space for a very long time. I have learned how to get out of such situations, and now I help other people to do the same.

Often, the question is why? Why do we choose to stay? For myself, staying was about supporting other people and not leaving anyone behind. Supporting my husband at the time or supporting family members to help them realise their dreams because I always felt that I knew where I was going in life, and nobody wants to excel and grow on their own. You want to bring people with you on your journey. You tend to not want to succeed and become abundant and wealthy, and be on your own. I would often ask why anyone would want to do that.

However, I soon realised that some journeys you have to do on your own because ultimately, having gone through various experiences, the way I live my life now I have created a blueprint for other people to see how something can be done, but I had to initially step out and do it on my own.

I mentioned before that, once you get clarity, you then have your choices, and once you know what your choices are, then you have to forgive yourself. I have an exercise where I do mirror work with my clients.

When coaching people, I ask my clients to look at themselves in a mirror for a few minutes in silence. You'd be surprised the number of people who do not look at themselves in the mirror. I encourage them to look in the mirror as they repeat aloud statements of forgiveness and promises.

For example,

'I am Jeanna Adowa Brodie-Mends and I forgive you for allowing yourself to stay in that rabbit hole. I forgive you for limiting yourself. I forgive you for dimming your light or not allowing yourself to shine, not using your voice, not using your choices.'

And then there are the promises,

The Journey Before Success

'Jeanna Adowa Brodie-Mends, I promise you that I will use my voice to fulfil my purpose. I promise you that I will love you unconditionally and never give up, no matter what. I promise to live life on my own terms ...'

This exercise always has tears, shock and then laughter. I encourage you to do this exercise in your own time.

See the link at the back of this toolkit to get your free downloadable PDF to support you to do this exercise.

Being comfortable in the rabbit hole

The rabbit hole was not safe because I wasn't in a good place. It was not violent in any way; when I say not safe, I mean in terms of my physical and emotional health. I was in my comfort zone and was very complacent. When you have given so much of you to others, often there is no more left to give to yourself.

I felt like I was running at 10% capacity of who I actually was, while I had unconsciously given 90% of me away.

Burn those ships

The Journey Before Success

Have you heard the story of the Emperor who takes his soldiers to war? During their journey at sea, the Emperor saw that they were becoming weary and fear was setting in. While they were on the shoreline, the Emperor noticed the fear and anxiety increasing. The Emperor ordered his fire bearers to shoot arrows at the ships out at sea, blowing them all up.

Why does he do this? To make the soldiers realise that there is no going back – they either win this war and get through or they die. I love that analogy, especially when people take the initial step, because you have to get very non-negotiable with what it is that you're choosing to go forward with.

For me, I had to become non-negotiable throughout 2016. I burned those ships when I chose to take the decision to go to Dubai. I burned those ships because I knew that, when I returned, I would come back to a whole lot of chaos and nonsense. People say, 'How could you do that?' Still, I knew I was moving forward, and I was not prepared to go back or stay in that space. I burned those ships in 2016, and I haven't turned back. I continued to move forward on my Journey Before Success; it was the beginning of my transformation for me.

The Journey Before Success

"'For I know the plans I have for you," declares the Lord, "plans to prosper you and not to harm you, plans to give you a hope and a future."' – Jeremiah 29:11

One of my go-to scriptures.

The Journey Before Success

Call to action

Now it is time to do the internal work and get some clarity. Get your journal and answer the following questions as truthfully as possible.

1. Describe where you are right now in your life. Identify any areas you want to improve.

2. Write down who you want to become.

3. Identify YOUR Babu moment when you realised something had to change.

4. List three choices you will take to improve your current situation.

5. As you end this chapter, I would encourage you to reflect on how far you have come. Although you are not where you want to be, appreciate that you are not where you used to be. You have started YOUR Journey Before Success and are doing the work to become the truest and highest expression of yourself.

Dwenninmmen

(Ram's Horn)
Humility and Strength

You have no power in any other territory
other than your own!
– Oprah Winfrey

The Journey Before Success

The Journey Before Success

Lesson 2:
The Power of Your Voice... (Affirmations)

It is a common stereotype that Black people do not swim. A stereotype? I don't think it is one, because it is the reality for a lot of Black females. I have found over the years that we do not want to go swimming because of our hair. We make comments such as 'oh my gosh, the chlorine will damage my hair' or 'my hair will get too frizzy'. There is always a reason.

Parents would say, 'Oh my gosh. I have to do your hair again! I think we should just relax your hair.' Now we know how bad that can be.

However, as I like to travel, I love the idea of swimming. When I was younger, probably from the age of 7, I went swimming with my school; swimming lessons were once a week. Despite attending these lessons until I was 12 years old I still didn't learn to swim. I would be in the water, doing whatever I was doing, but I just wasn't swimming.

As an 18-year-old, I knew that I wanted to travel the world, who I was and what I wanted to do with my life. I had the revelation that my life was going to be that of a woman who travels around the world and wasn't really focused on building a

The Journey Before Success

family home and having children. I wanted to travel and connect with many cultures, places and things.

I had to ask myself, 'Jeanna, if you travel around the world, when you go on the boats or ships and want to jump in the sea, how would you do this when you can't swim?' I decided to pay for swimming lessons. I was worried, thinking, 'Oh my gosh, for many years, I didn't learn to swim. Am I really going to learn?'

At this time, I was slightly overweight but not too much. Still, I worried about the swimming costume and how I looked. I was in the changing room, where I had to shower before entering the swimming pool. I was looking through the glass when I caught a glimpse of the instructor.

Shock, horror! The instructor was the same instructor I had had since age 7. My heart started to pound because I'm thinking, 'Oh my gosh, it's him.' I waited for other people to go out before walking through the door. He looked at me and went red in the face, starting to swear, and began shouting at me from across the pool. I stopped in my tracks as he said, 'Get down here, get down here.' 'I'm not doing this. I'm not f@*%ing doing this!' he said, shouting at the top of his lungs.

Everyone is now just staring at me and thinking, what is going on here? 'Get in the water!' he said, but I just looked at him, wondering if he was mad. He was in the deep end, asking me to get in there. 'If you do not get in the water, I'm going to push you in,' he said.

At that moment, all I heard was that someone was going to remove my choice. I jumped in the water, and then he said, 'Right! Get down to the other end,' and I swam to the shallow end. When I stood up, everyone was clapping for me. I looked back and had a *Babu moment* as I realised I could actually swim.

I share this story to show what happens when we recognise the power of having our right to choose. Knowing that someone could remove that power from me made me jump, although afraid. Sometimes, we say things without realising what it will take to get there.

I wanted to know how to swim to live the lifestyle of my dreams – the lifestyle that I wanted. Yet, was I really prepared to go through what it would take? And I ask people the same question: are you really prepared to go through what it would take to achieve the goals you have set for your life?

It's key to have a second set of eyes. The instructor who recognised me from when I was aged 7, learning to swim through secondary school, knew that I had the ability to swim. However, for whatever reason, I did not swim. He was never going to push me into a situation where I would drown.

A second set of eyes is one of the key benefits of having a coach. A coach can see things that you can't see, and when you say you want to achieve something, they can see that you can already do it, so they will push you that bit extra to get you to that point. When I coach people, I ask them, what is your affirmation?

What words do you stand on?

Let me share with you some of the affirmations I have on my vision board that I see and can read daily.

I Live in Peace, Love and Prosperity
I Am Aligned
I Am Power
I Am Financially Abundant
I Am Safe
I Am Love
I Am Africa

The Journey Before Success

Call to action

Now it is time to do your internal shadow (mirror) work:

1. What messaging have you received that has limited your ability to be your true self?

2. List some of the experiences you have missed out on as a consequence of negative messaging.

3. What experiences would you like to have but still feel limited to experience today?

4. What messaging can you use to create a positive shift in your mindset moving forward?

5. Affirmations are a good tool that I use on my Journey Before Success. Write down at least 3 affirmations that you commit to implementing for the next 30 days on your own journey.

6. If you use social media, why not take it a step further and post your affirmations and tag us @annaej_coaching in your post? Let us be a part of your journey and be a second set of eyes.

The Journey Before Success

Ananse Ntontan

Like a spider web on our Journey,
we must apply **Wisdom and Creativity** and
appreciate the **Complexities** of life. Through
all things, we must give thanks.

The Journey Before Success

Lesson 3:
Gratitude is a Must

I always encourage people to give thanks before even getting out of bed. When I wake up, I give thanks to the Almighty Creator, my ancestors and Spirit. I go through a whole series of acknowledgements and giving thanks. Rather than say 'good morning,' I say 'grand rising.' I am very particular about the words I use. So I say grand rising because I am waking up to a grandiose day.

I keep a gratitude journal, and I encourage all my clients and anyone who will listen to get a gratitude journal. Write down the things you are grateful for at the start of the day and again at the end of the day; write down things that you're grateful you have achieved throughout the day. It could be something that made you smile or someone with whom you had a nice conversation. It could have been a meal that you prepared and ate or the enjoyment you received from the environment(s) you were in.

It is important to always give thanks and show gratitude on your Journey Before Success. It is like with children – when you praise a child, a child repeats what they have done. When you set goals and you have been implementing them and taking actions, achieving goals, no matter how small or big, and you show gratitude for that, chances are

The Journey Before Success

you are going to repeat it again and again. This gives you the satisfaction that you're on the right track.

Once you build this into a practice that you have, you will be looking for things to be grateful for because you're going to want to have something to write in your journal.

Journals are a very useful tool that I refer to as an emotional bank account that can be a source of encouragement when you are going through the storms of life. You can pick up your journal and sit in your quiet place and read all that you have achieved and have been grateful for to date.

This has served me and many of my clients on our journey, as when we are in the storm we may not be able to see or think clearly.

Do you know whose words we believe above anyone else's? Our own.

It's your words that you will read and use to bring you back to where you need to be.

We all need to have an emotional bank account.

'Operate on the right frequency and remain focused on the light and positive energy when the darkness appears.' – Jeanna

The Journey Before Success

Call to action

Now it is time to open your own bank account:

1. Outline your morning routine.

2. List seven things in your journal that you have achieved that you are grateful for.

3. Now put on a song, and dance and celebrate yourself!

   A song I do this to is Diana Ross's *I'm Coming Out*. Dance like no one is watching you and go for it. Do this at least once a week, because what is celebrated gets repeated.

   Keep going!!!

The Journey Before Success

Nea Onnim No Sua A Ohu

Lifelong Learning

We must all have a continued desire to learn and develop our knowledge and skills.

We do not get different results while we remain in the same space.
– Jeanna

The Journey Before Success

The Journey Before Success

Lesson 4:
Cultivating Your Purpose

Purpose gives people choices, and knowing your purpose helps you to keep on track. Your purpose will get you up in the morning and give you a reason to get out of bed. Knowing your purpose is your motivation for your why.

I am often referred to as a watcher of people and tasked with showing people how to use their voices. I know my purpose is to show people how to break down complex situations and set achievable goals.

Knowing this encourages me to wake up every morning as I know someone is waiting on me to show up as my authentic self. My purpose encourages me to be open-minded and solution-focused during my coaching sessions as I already know that every client is going to be unique.

My purpose offers me vision and direction, prompting me to offer different approaches, workshops both on and offline. A key model I use is 'Know Yourself To Lead Yourself' as this tool encourages me to truly appreciate how my tendencies and patterns of behaviour contribute to my actions on a daily basis. My actions have direct consequences and this becomes my reality.

The Journey Before Success

I know I have to know myself to lead myself and others, and you need to know the same – as your beliefs, actions, habits and patterns of behaviours become your reality.

My purpose and my crown are one and the same.

When people look at who I am as a person, they should also see that my purpose is a crown I wear. Yes, my title is a Strategic Coach, but my purpose and my crown are one and the same.

Typically, I ask people, 'Are you a Moses or a Joshua?' And for people unfamiliar with the narrative, Moses' purpose was to take the children of Israel out from Egypt into the promised land, but Moses had areas of reluctance and self-doubt and so God provided Joshua to walk alongside Moses on the journey.

Joshua, being more bold and confident, knew his assignment and executed it. As a result it was Joshua who led the people into the promised land, whereas Moses saw the promised land, but did not enter it.

(This is a very brief summary and my interpretation; you may want to read the full story further.)

The Journey Before Success

Are you a Moses or a Joshua? The difference is in knowing your purpose, knowing your why, knowing the method you're going to use to get your desired outcomes.

Although Moses knew his purpose, and I guess he probably knew his why, the method wasn't applied as instructed and the outcomes weren't achieved because he didn't get into the promised land.

The Journey Before Success

Call to action

How well do you know yourself to lead yourself?

Let's identify your purpose:

1. Ask yourself, what you would do every day if money was not a concern? This will be your purpose and your why.

2. Demonstrate how often you live your purpose in your everyday life. Write a few examples.

3. Have you been a Moses or a Joshua? Be honest.

4. List your desired outcomes moving forward.

5. Describe what action steps you will take to implement your purpose.

Nkyimu

Use skill and precision at all times.

If you fail to plan, you plan to fail.
– La Braya

The Journey Before Success

The Journey Before Success

Lesson 5:
Strategic Planning

Before you start a journey, you need to know your destination. There is no point wandering down the road on a journey when you have no clue of where you're trying to get to. You need a plan.

The question is, where are you trying to get to? Your plan helps you identify and keep you on track with your chosen goals.

It's important that we focus on intentional goal setting and the need to take decisive action. This lesson will discuss the importance of knowing your macro and micro goals and their differences.

Now let's be clear, macro goals are your big goals. With my JBS clients this would be either their 5-, 3- or 1-year goals as an initial assessment and in the construction of their journey planner.

For this lesson we will use 90 days as our macro goal and 30 days as our micro goals. These are the smaller goals you will identify and implement that are a direct link to achieving your overall 90-day macro goals.

When I coach, I encourage my clients to be very intentional when defining their goals, to be very clear on what they actually want to achieve.

The Journey Before Success

What is their macro goal? What do they want to achieve within the next 90 days? I encourage my clients to make it something that pushes them out of their comfort zone, not just something that is easily achievable; otherwise, there will be no growth.

Now let's face it, a plan without action is merely a dream. Taking action is taking an active step to bring your vision to life.

Your action plan will involve listing exactly how you will actively achieve these goals.

I tend to take a 90-day approach to achieving desired goals. I break the year into four seasons – spring (planning, sowing), summer (nurturing, harvest), autumn (harvest), winter (dormant, rest, evaluation, planning) – and I encourage my clients to work in 90-day cycles.

Now remember your macro goal is the 90-day goal you are trying to achieve. For example, one of my macro goals was to release 1 ½ stones in weight (and I say release weight because the weight I release I am not trying to get back, so I don't say lose weight).

The Journey Before Success

This is how I break down the macro goal into bite-sized achievable steps.

For example,

I have decided that my goal is to release 1 ½ stones over 90 days. I will then decide: 'Each month – 30 days – my goal is to release seven pounds of weight.' That is half a stone each month.

By the end of 90 days I should have achieved my desired weight release goal of 1 ½ stones gone.
I use weight as an example because everyone seems to be able to identify with it. Already knowing my macro and micro goals, the action I would take is to ensure that I have physical activity at least 3–4 times a week.
I will ensure that I meal prep and wake up early. That is my action plan.
I can say that I did this and was able to release 2 ½ stones in a 90-day period. YES! I shocked myself.

Remember you can use your journal to write your goal for the day and celebrate your wins in your gratitude journal.

It is key on your journey to evaluate and reflect on your achievements once you have completed both your 30-day and 90-day goals and make the necessary adjustments before you begin another cycle of 90 days.

The Journey Before Success

This too shall pass

There is a story of a king who was going to war. However, he was somewhat worked up and a bit anxious, so he called on his trusted advisers. Although they tried, he could not be calmed; his anxiety levels were still high.

Then he remembered a person who worked within the palace and called for him. The king asked this man, 'Do you have any words of encouragement for me before I go to battle or words you would like to share?' The man wrote something down on a piece of paper, rolled it up and asked the king to put it in his ring. Then the man said, 'Only when you get to a point you feel you cannot do anything more should you open it and read the message.'

Now the king had gone out to battle and arrived at a point where it seemed there was no way out. His enemies had closed him in from every direction and he thought this was it. This was where he and the rest of his men would die. Suddenly he remembered the message; he opened it up and read it. The message read: 'This too shall pass.' At that moment, the message spoke to his purpose, causing the king to think: 'Find a way. Just find a way to get through this. You will be all right.' And with that Babu moment, his shift in mindset, the king said, 'Yes! This too shall pass indeed.'

The Journey Before Success

The king was peaceful enough to think about his skills and why he had set off on the journey in the first place. He knew what he was meant to be doing and took decisive action.

They won that battle and returned to the palace, celebrating. The king saw the man and called out to him, saying, 'We won! We won! This is so great, it's fantastic. Do you have a word of encouragement for me? Or do you have a message for me?' The man said to the king, 'Read the message.' Without a second thought, the king opened his ring and read the message. Again, it said: 'This too shall pass.' The king looked at the man and nodded in understanding.

The reason I share this story is so you understand that life happens. We have our ups, and we have our downs; that is just life. Failures will come, but ultimately our failures are our greatest teachers in life. There will be moments when we celebrate and enjoy and other times when we have to ask ourselves: 'How the hell did that happen!'

In all things, be grateful that you have the opportunity to either learn or thrive. Remember your *journey* is not solely about the end destination; rather, it's about appreciating the process.

The Journey Before Success

With my weight goal, I constantly seek fun activities to keep me physically active. What creative meal prep can I come up with to enjoy it? It is not just about getting to the end goal. I want to live my life, not simply endure it, and I encourage you to do the same.

Celebrate your wins daily, and this means being grateful because gratitude is celebration. Keeping a gratitude journal is helpful because when people feel low, as was the case for millions of people who were isolated and lonely during the COVID pandemic, those who kept a journal could look back at their journey during the pandemic.

Since they have had the opportunity to come through the trauma of the pandemic and be able to sit down and review their own story and not someone else's, it is a good way to help them and us all realise that actually, despite the storms that rage around us, this too shall pass.

The Journey Before Success

Call to action

Let's be intentional with your Journey planner:

1. Reflect and describe the season you are currently in.

2. List your 3–5 maximum macro goals for the next 90 days.

3. Break your macro goals into smaller bite-sized micro goals that you will need to implement daily to achieve your goals.

4. Now go and take action. Remember the story of the king when you face any challenges on your journey and when you have success. Life is a journey; we will experience both ups and downs.

The Journey Before Success

The feeling of the first tentacle rubbing my clit combined with the second pressed against his cock inside my hot channel is already so intense. When that third one works its way into my tight asshole, I just explode.

I am rubbed, rutted, worked on, and writhed against and it's beyond overwhelming. Ori groans as I squeeze, pulse, and shudder through my climax. His eyes can't stop flitting back and forth between my face and the place where he's fucking me. I finally manage to lift myself enough to look at what's going on down there and catch a glimpse of the tentacle rubbing my clit.

It's white, and smooth, and fuck *it's so weird, right*? But *damn* it feels good.

Suddenly the tentacles snap out of existence, or absorb back into his body, I'm not really sure. All I know is they're gone fast. I yelp with surprise. I'm left with my beautiful Ori, and his made-to-order cock. He kisses me deeply, running his fingers through my hair over and over before pulling back and rutting hard into me.

"*Oh*, Anne," Ori chokes out. "I'm going to come."

"Then come, please, fill me up."

I'm assuming he can't get me pregnant, so the whole breeding kink thing will be alright, right?

"You don't understand." His face screws up and he

pulls out of me with a hiss, holding his cock above me.

Okay, coming on my chest is fine too. I close my eyes and wait for the onslaught of jizz...but it doesn't come.

When I hear him gasp and moan my name, I cautiously open my eyes. Something tickles my stomach and I give an incredulous snort as I see the white, fluffy things in the air.

I lift my head to see a final spurt of downy feathers float out from the end of his cock. They're everywhere in the air between us, landing on my nude body, my face, my hair.

I begin to laugh; I can't control it.

The blissed-out look on Ori's face falls at the sound of my laughter. *Oh no.* He slides backward on the bed, away from me.

"No, no, I'm not laughing at you. Come here, please." I hold out my arms and wait, hoping he isn't too upset.

After a moment his look softens and he settles into my arms, head on my shoulder. "You promise you don't think I'm disgusting? I didn't think about what would happen until I was nearly there and then it hit me. All that's inside me that would come out are feathers."

"Disgusting? How could I think you're disgusting?

The feathers are so sweet! I laughed because of how much joy it brought me, not because I was making fun of you or something." I rub my face into his hair. "It's just another way you're perfect for me. It means you can never get me pregnant and since I absolutely do not want to ever get knocked-up that's like a huge plus."

I nip his ear and he laughs before settling his head on my chest.

"You're in charge of sweeping up all the mess though."

"Gladly. If a bit of housework is the only sacrifice I need to make to make love to the most beautiful woman on the planet, then so be it."

"You know, you haven't really met any other women."

"I don't need to. I've seen them on the internet when you're browsing it."

"Oh boy. You have a lot to learn. What am I going to do with you?" I ruffle his hair and giggle, thinking of all the things I'm going to have to teach him.

"Well, hopefully more sex. And you'll need to take me to buy at least one more pillow, as a replacement you know, since you're one short. For me to use, not you. You have me."

I roll my eyes. "Okay, Ori. Let's get a little rest and after that we'll learn about the world beyond the internet."

Chapter 16

Ori

"And this is a kitten. Personally, my pet of choice. They're just so fuzzy-wuzzy."

My Anne and I are at the animal rescue shelter picking out a pet. She's wanted one for a while, and I need company while she's at work, so we think a pet might be good for us.

I'm not quite at the social level to venture into the world on my own for long periods of time yet so I'm stuck at home without Anne during the day. I really don't mind; it's not as if that wasn't my reality for my entire existence prior to becoming a man. It will be nice to have another living being around though, I will admit. I have a great urge to serve and care for Anne, as she's the whole reason I'm alive. When she's not around, it will be good to use some of that energy to take care of a being that was abandoned and needs it desperately.

"Here, you hold the kitty." Anne passes the wriggling kitten to me, and I wrap it in my arms.

It really is a wonderful creature, so soft and full of

life. I scratch the top of its tiny gray head and it vibrates with a purr. My face cracks wide in a smile. The kitten kneads my arm until its claw catches on my fabric and tears a small hole. I don't bleed but a small puff of feathers floats through the air. The kitten sits up to bat at them.

I quickly hand the feline back to Anne, who looks around the room to make sure no one has seen what just happened. Thankfully no one has.

"Well, perhaps we should get a hamster instead. Or a fish."

I feel bad, crushing her kitten dreams. But Anne simply laughs.

"It's alright Ori, I think fish are pretty cool, too."

The next day we finished setting up our goldfish. Anne goes to work. The sweet little swimmer was a great choice. It's a lovely fish, and we picked a great big tank, so it has a lot of room to swim around. Apparently the person who had the fish before us kept it in a tiny bowl, which is quite sad, so I'm glad to give it a new life.

A knock on the door startles me, interrupting my enjoyment of Carl, which is what we named the fish.

I open the door and find none other than the landlord, an absolute asshole. He's been bothering Anne about me staying at the apartment, and finally forced her to pay extra for me to stay here. I have no idea what he wants now.

"Yes, James?" I drawl.

"I've said twenty times now, it's Jimmy. Just checking on the place, seeing you ain't got no more people staying here." He looks past me into the apartment.

"I assure you we have no one else here. Have a fine day now." I move to close the door, but *Jimmy* puts his Croc-wearing foot in the way.

"Not so fast. I see you got a pet now. That means a pet fee. That's a pet deposit plus pet rent each month." He grins as he scratches a sweaty armpit. "Gonna need that right away, fancy boy."

"It's a fish, *Jimmy*. I'm sure you don't need all of that." I say through clenched teeth.

Jimmy pushes past me into the apartment and I can feel a hot rage burning in my chest.

"Well, if you got a fish you might have something else. Let's see. You got a dog? A cat? Cat fee is extra seeing as they stink up the place and all."

He starts to head toward the bedroom. *Absolutely not.*

I take a step to follow him, but my leg gives out.

Damn it!

I haven't told Anne yet, but it appears I need to feed to keep up my life force. Those first times weren't enough; I need regular maintenance. I can't eat *food*, we've discovered, unfortunately, so that's no help. I need to drain life. I've been carefully skimming tiny bits from rude people when we've gone out without telling Anne, but everyone has been so pleasant lately. *Fuck.*

I rub my leg until I can limp along enough behind the landlord. By this time, he's made it to Anne's room and is bent over, searching under her bed.

"I don't see no cat but that don't mean you won't get one, so I'll be back soon," he says as he stands up.

I grab him by his thick, sweaty throat.

"I don't believe you will, James. I don't believe you'll bother me or my precious Anne ever again."

I begin to drain his life force slowly, relishing the feel of taking revenge on this parasite. I watch as he turns gray, feel my leg become stronger as he does. Before I am able to take all his life I stop, letting go of his throat. He falls, but I catch his limp form.

"No, you won't be coming back, will you?" I smile, pinching his sagging cheek.

As I leave the apartment I check to make sure the stairwell is empty, then carry James to the bottom of the stairs, where I leave him seated, drooling, propped carefully so he won't fall. Someone will find him eventually and take him somewhere safe, I'm sure.

I return to the apartment and watch Carl again, happily swimming in his big tank. I feel a strange sensation on my wrist and lift my sleeve to see what's going on. *Oh no.*

Flesh. Real flesh.

It appears I took too much life force and started to become more *man* than pillow. This simply won't do. Anne won't like this one bit. I run to the bedroom and remove my clothes, checking in the mirror to see if any other parts of me have turned to flesh. Thankfully there aren't any. I sigh in relief.

When Anne returns I carefully avoid letting her touch that particular area on my wrist. It will take a while for my life energy to fade down enough for that to go away but I'm sure it will. For now, I'll just be careful she doesn't touch it.

As for James, he was gone when she arrived, and no one came knocking at our door to ask any questions. Perfect.

"Darling, are you hungry? Do you want me to order you some tacos? Curry?" I ask my sweet Anne as I rub her feet.

She had a tough day at work, and I want to make sure she's as comfortable at home as she can be.

"Oh no, I'm good. I had some pizza at work for some dumb pizza party they threw as a bonus instead of actually giving us a raise. So, I'm stuffed."

My lip quirks up at the side. I lean back on our new pillow, one stuffed with artificial material—I don't trust feathers—and grin broadly at my Anne.

"Actually, I believe I'm the one that's stuffed."

Thank you to Latrexa, Vera, Tawny, Shannon, and everyone else who helped make this story possible. You are the best of people, flesh or fabric.

Printed in Great Britain
by Amazon

32397900R00046